THE WISDOM OF NATURE

FOR EDWIN, PTOLEMY,
OLIVIA AND RABBIT

THE WISDOM OF NATURE

INSPIRING LESSONS
FROM THE UNDERDOGS OF THE
NATURAL WORLD TO MAKE LIFE
MORE OR LESS BEARABLE

DIXE WILLS

ILLUSTRATED BY KATIE PONDER

Hardie Grant

QUADRILLE

'YOU'
ALMOST
WHO
A GOO
TO
ABOUT

L FIND
NO ONE
HAS
WORD
SAY
RABIES.'

CONTENTS

INTRODUCTION

'If only Mother Nature could speak some Human language,' we sigh. 'Just think how much wisdom she could impart to us.'

This is true, of course. And if there were someone called Mother Nature, she would no doubt be desperate to pick up one of our languages (I'm guessing one of those with a lot of clicking might appeal to her) or for us to learn hers.

That is not to say that Humans have not made extensive efforts over the years to make out what she might actually be communicating to us. Take the Doctrine of Signatures. This was an attempt to wheedle out the secret messages sent to us via plant life by a Creator God. It was largely based on the supposed similarities between certain aspects of plants and parts of the Human body, and the belief that the properties of the plant were linked in some healing way with the things they resembled. Thus the brain-like Walnut was thought to be good for curing cerebral disorders.

Remarkably, it did actually work in one or two cases. The Foxglove bears obviously heart-shaped fruit, which, according to the precepts of the Doctrine of Signatures, made it effective in the treatment of coronary complaints. Curiously, that proved to be exactly the case: Foxgloves were the original source of digitalis (now synthetically produced), a drug that stimulates the heart muscle.

Turning the concept around by 180°, Victorian Humans, who were an odd lot, thought it a lot of fun to make Flora speak a language foisted upon them. They gave meanings to scores of flowers and plants and produced dictionaries setting them all out. The Language of Flowers was a convoluted affair, but those who took the trouble to learn it could send complicated and sometimes nuanced messages to their loved ones, ex-loved ones, and sworn enemies simply by sending them a bouquet of flowers or a plant.

A pink Carnation, for example, signified 'a woman's love'. Woe betide you if you received yellow ones though, because these expressed 'disdain'. The whole gamut of emotions, intentions and frosty reproaches could be unleashed in non-verbal form: 'love' (Rose), 'hatred' (Basil), 'revenge' (Birdsfoot Trefoil), 'cold-heartedness' (Lettuce), 'stupidity' (Horseshoe-leaf Geranium) and even 'ill-timed wit' (Sorrel). Some flowers conveyed whole sentences. Send someone a Chilean Bellflower, for example (we've all done it at some point), and you were putting across the idea that, 'There is no unalloyed good,' which is certainly one to get the heart thumping. A Clarkia, on the other hand, let the recipient know that, 'The variety of your conversation delights me.' Sadly, there does not appear to be a flower that meant, 'Don't patronise me, you pea-brained clown.'

The Doctrine of Signatures is clearly all rot (the flukey Foxgloves notwithstanding) and the Language of Flowers says a lot about the astonishing level of sexual repression prevalent in Victorian society but very little else. It's just as well, therefore, that at least there is one book (this one) that explains the gobbets of wisdom that Mother Nature is trying to communicate if only we could take them in. And because she's

Mother Nature, and thus a big fan of the downtrodden, she does it by means of all those creatures, plants and things that are neither creatures nor plants (we're looking at you, Fungi [page 122] and Lichen [page 144]) that we either detest, denigrate, or merely disregard.

Take the Cockroach (page 12), for example. Though we view it with a degree of disgust, it's a creature that will certainly have the last laugh in the event of nuclear war. Who better to learn from about playing the long game? The Rabies Virus (page 20), on the other hand, is infinitesimally small and yet has the intelligence to control its victims' behaviour in ways that will ensure its own continued existence. Is it therefore beyond us, as Humans with brains that are quite enormous, to come up with some quite good ideas for things? Dandelions (page 24), meanwhile, can teach us the power of tolerance and acceptance; Wasps (page 26) can be instructive with regards to criticism and our response to it; and Rats (page 30) show us a fine example of how to get on in life.

It's my hope that, with this book in your hand, you'll be inspired by the underdogs of the natural world and, from them, discover wisdom that will make your life more or less bearable. If it doesn't, try Walnuts – they *really* do look very much like brains, don't they?

DIXE WILLS
2019

COCKROACH

This six-legged insect with its long antennae and rolled-up-newspaper-defying exoskeleton is an object of almost universal disgust. It's a sure sign that you need to overthrow your own government when its leaders start labelling as Cockroaches some group or other that is supposedly responsible for all the ills of the nation. It's no wonder, then, that this ubiquitous member of the order Blattodea positively welcomes the onset of a global nuclear holocaust, safe in the knowledge that it will be one of the few life forms to survive the ensuing hugger-mugger. Furthermore, Cockroaches have been around for at least 320 million years, can survive by eating the glue off the back of postage stamps, have been known to live for several hours after decapitation, and have given birth in space – feats that have thus far proved beyond the capacity of so-called *Homo sapiens*. And to cap it all, each Cockroach has eighteen knees. Take that, feeble duo-kneed Humans.

NATURE'S LESSON

Play the long game. Cockroaches may be the underdog right now but they don't lose their heads over it. And even if they do lose their heads, they still don't let it cramp their style unduly. Thus, if anyone calls you a Cockroach, wear the insult with pride.

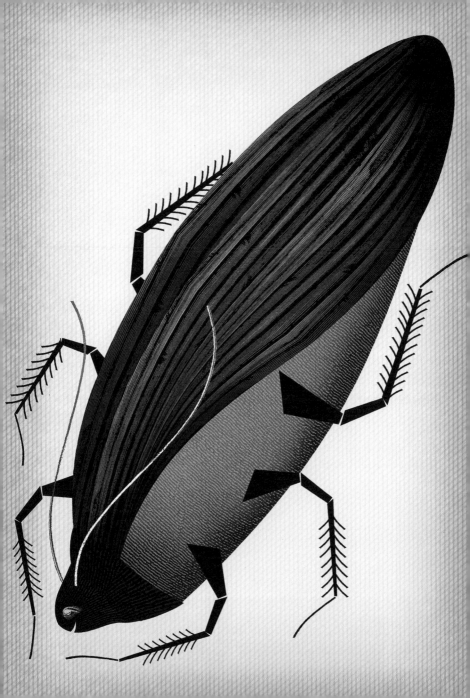

FOX

When, for hundreds of years, your species' primary cause of death is being torn apart by packs of Dogs for the amusement of the lowest form of Human life, it's all too easy to become depressed. However, forced from his rural setting to seek safety in towns and cities, the Fox had a pleasant surprise. Not only did the urban dwellers show no interest in chasing after him, but they left out food each night. This was contained in large receptacles topped with loose-fitting lids or in easy-rip, Fox-friendly bags specially designed for oral opening and being dragged about a bit. An unwritten law forbidding the depositing of such bags without first filling them with the carcass of at least one Chicken and the remains of various take-aways has given rise to the artistic school known as Vulpine Expressionism. The Expressionist Fox spurns traditional notions of the aesthetic, dispersing chicken bones and the residuum of pizzas in wide arcs and irregular lines on thoroughfares, gardens and unwary Cats. Like all great art movements, it is misunderstood.

NATURE'S LESSON

If you are forced to flee persecution, take heart: your traumatic experiences will form the fertile soil in which your creativity will flourish.

SLUG

'Homeless Snail', 'tube of slime', 'ectoplasm made flesh' – if ever
there were a creature in need of a top-flight PR agency it is the Slug.
And yet these put-upon creatures are more like Humans than we
might care to imagine: not only do they have a lung and kidneys
but, like most Humans, a heart too. Despite this, for many centuries,
these semi-humanoids were swallowed whole as a remedy for a
wide range of ailments such as toothache, warts and tuberculosis.
Nowadays the Slug's fate, all too often, is a more prosaic rubbing out
at the hands of some unfeeling gardener. If they're lucky, this entails
being split in twain by a well-aimed spade or poisoned like some
hapless victim in an Agatha Christie novel. But more terrible by
far is death by salt – the napalm of the Slug world – for this process
draws out all the moisture from within the poor beast, literally
desiccating it alive. No one wants that.

NATURE'S LESSON
Slugs, like us, yearn to be the object of a little Human love and
sympathy. Unlike Slugs, you have a chance of this dream coming
true. Also, beer will not kill you. Not immediately, anyway.

STICK

An apparently uncertain thing is the Stick. The poor man's coffee frother and perennial butt of the 'What's brown and sticky?' joke, a Stick has none of the dignity of the Twig, Branch or Bough. Though nominally resembling higher Stick-like forms such as Stick Insects, conductors' batons or, from a distance, the Apollo 13 rocket, nobody really knows where Sticks come from or indeed cares enough to ask. Does this get the Stick down? Far from it. When nobody's watching, all the planet's Sticks simply edge towards the nearest stream-spanning footbridge in the hope that they will be chosen to take part in a game of Poohsticks. This is the ultimate self-actualisation of the Stick and it is important to note that, just like the Olympics in times gone by, it is the taking part in a Poohsticks race that is the important thing, so every Stick considers itself a winner.

NATURE'S LESSON

Even if no one knows quite what you are, you can still serve some purpose in life (though perhaps it's best to draw the line at being lobbed off a bridge).

RABIES VIRUS

Search the globe as sedulously as you like, you'll find almost no one who has a good word to say about rabies. The disease is caused by lyssaviruses, most notably the Rabies Virus, and once contracted, almost always ends in the demise of the victim. Before death occurs, the hapless sufferer may have experienced a headache, fever, insomnia, anxiety, paralysis, hallucinations, extreme fear and delirium before a coma puts an end to the misery. Famously, subjects may also experience hydrophobia – the old name for rabies – though a fear of water is the least of their problems by that stage. Each year, the disease accounts for around 17,000 Humans globally. Brilliantly, one of the reasons for the astonishing success of the Rabies Virus is that it is able to cause rabid Dogs to react to the disease either by biting people or by becoming extremely affectionate and licking their bipedal best friends. Since both of these actions can transmit the disease, the Rabies Virus neatly doubles its chances of being passed on to a Human. Not bad for something that is just 180 nanometres long.

NATURE'S LESSON

Despite being vanishingly small, the Rabies Virus still has the brains to devise a canny way of getting on in the world. The average Human brain is roughly 1.62 x 1034 times larger than the Rabies Virus. Surely you can think up something?

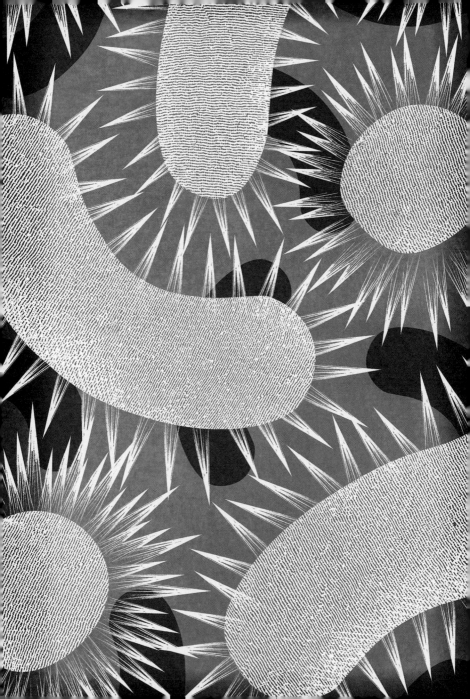

MOSS

Who would be Moss? You're not quite Grass (page 84) – indeed, you're hounded out of lawns with poison – and your wanton destruction is celebrated by no lesser light than Sir Elton Hercules John. 'I sat on the roof,' the Pinner-born septuagenarian croons before adding, with what one might consider unnecessary delight, 'and kicked off the Moss.' No matter that the words of his 1970 hit *Your Song* were written by Bernie Taupin, the message is all too clear that the only thing this small, flowerless, rootless plant is good for is as a provider of a slightly clunky means of conveying a sense of ennui and artistic dissatisfaction. Yet it behoves us to remember that the Mosses around us today are the ancestors of Algae that made an epoch-making journey from sea to land some 450 million years ago, heroically overcoming the twin difficulties of coping with gravity for the first time and not drying out. Quick as a flash (if a flash were to last millions of years) they evolved into Bryophytes, one of whose major strands is the Moss family. Some of those Mosses then went on to save countless lives in World War I, when used as an antiseptic dressing on wounds.

NATURE'S LESSON

Ignore Elton John. He knows nothing.

DANDELION

If only the Dandelion were not so fond of inhabiting gardens, it might today be cherished as a cheerful little wild flower, as dear to us as the Violet or the Primrose. Instead, it is dismissed as a weed and harassed at every turn. In an echo of Orwell's Big Brother declaring that Oceania had always been at war with Eurasia, it's popularly believed that gardeners have always been at daggers drawn with the Dandelion. However, sally back to the Middle Ages and you'll find the plant was actually cultivated for its leaves. These were commonly added to salads – they have a peppery flavour not unlike Rocket – or used by herbalists to treat skin diseases and rheumatism. Even today this persecuted member of the Daisy family sees service as a tea, a wine, a startlingly effective diuretic and as the inspiration for whatever synthetic flavouring mimics the first half of the soft drink 'Dandelion and Burdock'. If this were not enough, it is also possible to tell the time with a Dandelion by blowing its spherical seed head and counting the number of seeds that remain, thus saving the user the expense of a watch.

NATURE'S LESSON

Oceania has not always been at war with Eurasia – try to live and let live.

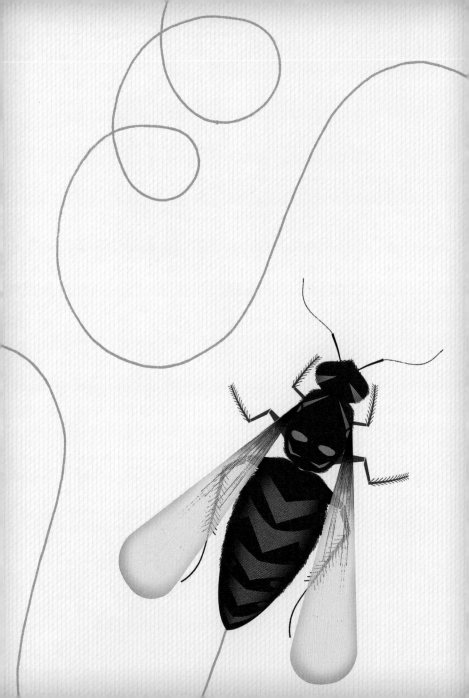

WASP

Bees, Bees, Bees – we all love Bees nowadays, albeit only because we discovered that if they all died out, Humankind would follow four years later. But what of their evil cousin, the Wasp? The perennial ruiner of picnics, *Vespula vulgaris* appears to have no redeeming qualities whatsoever and is feared and reviled in equal measure. Certainly, these little bundles of maliciousness and spite in insect form appear not to lose any sleep reflecting on the morality of their lifestyle choices. They kidnap insects and keep them imprisoned in the hive until they can be fed alive to their newly hatched young. The female Wasp, meanwhile, uses her sting to incapacitate animals so that she can lay her eggs inside them. Her venom releases a pheromone that makes other Wasps nearby become more aggressive towards perceived enemies and that same venom can also kill Humans who are susceptible to anaphylactic shock. It must be said that there is one species of Wasp that is vital to the pollination of Figs and another that makes crop-destroying Aphids (page 146) explode, but these are scorned by proper Wasps as effete liberal do-gooders.

NATURE'S LESSON

Ignore the critics – haters gonna hate. Also, yellow and black stripes are a strong look.

DESTROYING
ANGEL

The Quentin Tarantino of poisonous Fungi (page 122), the Destroying Angel not only possesses one of the most magnificent names ever bestowed upon a living thing, it is also extremely good at what it does: poisoning its adversaries. All white, as if butter wouldn't melt in its volva, the Destroying Angel is a wonderfully sculptural creation with an elegantly tall and slender stem. It is also one of the world's most toxic Fungi. It contains amatoxins so powerful that anyone who consumes a mere 0.1 milligram of the Mushroom for each kilogram of their bodyweight can expect a swift and unpleasant end. Furthermore, the Destroying Angel is a member of a maverick free-thinking group. Clearly not animals but not really proper plants either, Fungi have had to be classified by taxonomists as the only members of a wholly separate kingdom. But back to the killing. Over the course of its life cycle the Destroying Angel can be mistaken for three popular edible Fungi: the Puffball, Button Mushroom and Horse Mushroom. Once consumed, symptoms can take from five to 24 hours to materialise, by which time the effects on the liver and kidneys are usually irreparable. After a brief remission, those two organs typically fail, plunging the victim into a hepatic coma followed not long after by death.

NATURE'S LESSON

Whatever it is you do, be the best.

BROWN RAT

Famously, one of the many attractions of living in a large city is that one is never more than six feet from the nearest Rat. To be precise, that's the Brown Rat, whose scientific name, *Rattus norvegicus*, stems from the mistaken belief that the toothy little Muroid was originally a native of Norway (it probably comes from northern China). Nevertheless, the Rat has long been a synonym for a scoundrel, viz. 'a dirty Rat' or, in the peculiar parlance of the tabloid newspaper, 'a love Rat'; while 'to Rat on someone' is to betray them. This last usage is a particular calumny since Rats are not only extremely sociable animals, they are very loyal: for example, they take care of any injured or poorly Rats in their party as a matter of course. Naturally clean creatures – an extensive grooming regime is part of their daily routine – they also possess excellent memories, particularly when it comes to navigation. Intelligent and endowed with a keen sense of smell, Rats have even shown themselves capable of being trained to sniff out landmines. By craftily stowing away on seagoing vessels, they have now colonised every continent on the globe bar Antarctica, making the Brown Rat one of the most successful mammals ever to have lived. Not bad for a 12-ounce rodent from the sewers.

NATURE'S LESSON
Just like the Rat, no one ever got on in life by not leaving a sinking ship.

WORM

Forever destined to be 'got' by the early bird and often prefixed with 'miserable' when used as an insult, the Worm is a downtrodden creature both literally and figuratively. Even Shakespeare, who championed the Ant (page 78) and even had good words to say about Toads (page 88), was damning of the Worm. '*No longer mourn for me when I am dead/Than you shall hear the surly sullen bell/Give warning to the world that I am fled/From this vile world, with vilest worms to dwell*', he quilled rancorously in Sonnet 71. And yet, if anything, the many thousands of Worm species have proved themselves allies to Humankind. They burrow tirelessly away, loosening the soil and thus improving yields for farmers and gardeners alike. Furthermore, Worms boast not just one but two nervous systems and, when their relative size is taken into account, are reckoned to be about a thousand times more powerful than Humans. They have a capacity for memory and possess an almost god-like power: should their lower body be involved in a non-fatal accident, with some effort they can regenerate themselves, replacing wounded or even severed parts. And they do all this without bothering with details like ears or eyes.

NATURE'S LESSON
Eat dirt. It's the new Avocado.

TICK

Nobody likes a parasite. One that jams its mouthparts into mammals, birds and other unwary creatures, gorges itself on their blood and offers nothing in return but pathogens is unlikely ever to worm its way into anyone's affections. Ticks are the ultimate expression of the hanger-on and have been indulging in this freeloading behaviour ever since they evolved to a blood-only diet around 120 million years ago, so we're well past the time when it can be excused as an aberration. What might earn the world's grudging admiration is the head-spinning range of diseases that Ticks are able to communicate to their hosts. Victims may contract not only the potentially life-threatening Lyme disease but also a whole cornucopia of more exotic ailments, including babesiosis, Bourbon virus, Boutonneuse fever, bovine anaplasmosis, Crimean Congo haemorrhagic fever, ehrlichiosis, Flinders Island spotted fever, meningoencephalitis, Q fever, rickettsialpox, Rocky Mountain spotted fever, tularemia and typhus, depending on where in the world they happen to be and the type of Tick they are unfortunate enough to encounter. There's even a species called the Lone Star Tick, found principally in North America, whose speciality is passing on a bacterium that causes Humans to become allergic to red meat. And they say Americans don't do irony.

NATURE'S LESSON

Leeching off people and attempting to infect everyone you meet won't get you on anyone's Christmas card list. However, that does leave your mantelpiece free for other stuff.

WOODLOUSE

With its armour-like plating and mud-grey colouring, the Woodlouse has the appearance of a tiny dinosaur that was overlooked during the asteroid-inspired mass extinction event 65 million years ago. It may therefore come as a surprise to learn that these little arthropods, whom one does not naturally associate with the seashore, are actually crustaceans. Thus they are closer cousins to Crabs (page 80), Lobsters, Barnacles and the like than to their fellow land-based invertebrates. However, they do harbour an atavistic need for dampness, hence their predilection for rotting vegetation and habitats that are shielded from the sun. Ever the maverick, the Woodlouse has taken to breathing through its hind legs, because if that's the sort of thing you can do, why wouldn't you? Their most remarkable feature, however, is their phenomenal ability to incorporate heavy metals into their bodies at levels that would be exceedingly poisonous to humans. Scientists have discovered concentrations of copper, lead, zinc and cadmium in the digestive glands of Woodlice that account for seven per cent of their total body weight. Few other animals on the planet come anywhere close to showing such commitment to the snapping up of unconsidered minerals.

NATURE'S LESSON

Breathe through your legs. It clearly pays.

LIGHTNING

Coming in two basic guises – sheet and forked – the oft misspelt electrostatic discharge creates light, sound and occasionally terror (particularly if you're standing under trees or sitting in a metal tube at 40,000 feet). While 75 per cent of Lightning activity takes place in the form of sheet Lightning – which does not make contact with the ground – one in four flashes makes the short journey down to Earth. Lightning bolts can contain up to 100 million volts, which may seem quite frightening until one realises that that would only discharge enough electricity to power a mid-range hand blender at full tilt for about 426 years. When not being measured in terms of hand-blender usage, Lightning serves as a shorthand for illustrating the likelihood of an event: viz. the average person being x times more likely to be struck by Lightning than they are to win a particular lottery. However, since the chances of anyone actually knowing how likely it is that they will be struck by Lightning are probably as likely as the event itself, the comparison is perhaps not as handy as its users imagine. It also shows just how far Lightning has come down in the world, since in ages past it was considered to represent either a god or the action of a god in a whole swathe of cultures, from the Hindu, Ancient Greek and Mayan to the Aztec, Norse, Bantu and Finnish.

NATURE'S LESSON

Hand blenders use a lot more electricity than anyone ever thought. Buy a whisk.

FLEA

Fleas are the bane of many pet owners' lives – forming a seemingly unvanquishable army of elusive and spiteful troops whose generals can call upon apparently unlimited reinforcements. It's easy to forget, in the heat of the mental battle against scratching those bites on the ankle, that the Flea is a marvel of nature. For one thing, those unlimited reinforcements are only possible on account of its mastery of the art of reproduction. Female Fleas can lay 20 eggs in a day, and just two months later, given optimum conditions, those twenty offspring will number 20,000. And then there's the Flea's extraordinary leap. Their hind legs are multijointed and it uses them as levers to force itself into the ground. Spines on the legs and feet grip the surface before the Flea releases the pent-up energy like a coiled spring, leaping up to 200 times its own length. If a six-foot human were to do the same thing, they would be able to jump over five Sydney Opera Houses stacked one on top of the other, should the Australians ever get their act together and make that happen. What is perhaps even more remarkable is that a Flea springing from the ground can accelerate at around 4,000 feet/second², which is roughly 60 times the rate achieved by a space rocket at take-off. The engineering that makes that possible in such minute creatures is little short of miraculous. It's just a pity about all the biting.

NATURE'S LESSON

Jump as if no one is watching. Bite as if you'll never eat again. Procreate as if the world weren't facing a severe over-population crisis.

VACUUM

Famously abhorred by Nature, Vacuums have been a source of fear and fascination since their existence was debated by the philosophers of Ancient Greece. Though Aristotle (very much a non-believer) has been proved wrong, it's fair to say that Perfect Vacuums – spaces void of all matter – are rare indeed. Even if you were in a position to scoop up a cubic metre of outer space you'd still find a handful of hydrogen atoms loitering about in it. Much lower-quality 'Partial Vacuums' are more easily come by. For instance, one of the first durable Partial Vacuums was produced by Italian physicist and barometer-inventor Evangelista Torricelli in 1643. You can recreate his Vacuum by (carefully) filling a tall test tube with mercury, and then (even more carefully) tipping it upside down into a bowl. The space in the test tube no longer occupied by mercury is your Vacuum. If you happen to be able to trap an old-school alarm clock in that space, you'll enjoy the unsettling experience of watching it go off without hearing it make any noise at all, for sound does not travel in a Vacuum. The posters were true all along: in space, no one can hear you scream (though if it's any consolation, those few hydrogen atoms will in fact aid the transmission of a magnificently insignificant portion of your final desperate shriek).

NATURE'S LESSON

Be positive. Like a Vacuum, you might amount to little more than an absence of anything in particular, but at least you're not antimatter.

LEYLAND
CYPRESS

Less a tree and more the embodiment of the sheer selfishness of modern society, the *Leylandii* is perhaps the only large plant better known by the second half of its scientific name than by its common English handle. It also owes its existence to a somewhat freakish occurrence. In the late 1840s, John Naylor called in designer Edward Kemp to improve the gardens at his Leighton Hall estate in Powys, Wales. Kemp had many trees planted, including two Cypresses: a Monterey and a Nootka. These species have such disparate ranges that they would never usually come within 400 miles of each other in the wild but at Leighton Hall they were placed close together. In 1888, they happened to cross-fertilise and a whole new tree, the Leyland Cypress, came into being. Today, virtually every *Leylandii* in existence is a descendant of that Welsh couple. The tree's ability to tolerate high levels of salt and pollution has made it very popular on several continents, particularly around the coast, but it is the astonishing speed with which it grows that has brought it notoriety. A *Leylandii* can put on three feet a year and can grow to over 100 feet tall. As a result, it has caused tens of thousands of legal disputes between neighbours and at least one murder.

NATURE'S LESSON

The Grass might well be greener on the other side of the fence. But you can always make it shadier.

MINNOW

There's nothing like being a Minnow if you want to be condescended to. Without being an exceptionally small freshwater fish – Eurasian Minnow adults are around eight to ten centimetres and Sticklebacks can be much smaller – the name has somehow become a byword for supposed puniness, especially in relation to unfancied footballing nations who have had the audacity to qualify for a major championship. A lover of fast-flowing water, the Minnow can be seen in many a countryside stream, apparently oblivious to its belittled status amongst fish. However, examine one minutely and you'd discover two rather extraordinary things. First of all, the Minnow has teeth in its throat. Indeed, only in its throat. Even more unexpectedly, the fish is the possessor of an intricate bone structure connected to its inner ear that gives it an exceptionally well developed sense of hearing. It means it can pick up the jejune murmuring of anglers from some distance away. It can thus prevent itself from being hooked out of the water and used as bait for some larger prey, the ultimate in humiliating deaths.

NATURE'S LESSON

Rejoice in being a Minnow – aside from anything else, it seriously ups your chances of knocking out England in the quarter-finals.

GORSE

Best known for its tendency to claw at the clothes, skin, hair and patience of anyone incautious enough to attempt to plough through it – perhaps on some unwary mission to retrieve an errant frisbee or mislaid infant – Gorse is such a common sight that it is seldom noticed at all. However, without it, the Yellow-browed Warbler, the Whinchat and the Stonechat would have a hard time of it indeed, while many another small bird finds a secure home for its nest in the shrub's protecting screen of thorns. The Common Gorse, *Ulex europaeus*, also achieves the remarkable feat of bringing a hint of the Tropics to the most dismal heathland or desolate outcrop with its coconut-scented flowers. But it's the plant's curious relationship with fire that makes it really stand out. Gorse is highly flammable and positively encourages combustion. Rather than destroying the plant, flames aid its regeneration by helping to open its seed pods. After the fire, new shoots also appear rapidly from the blackened remains, whilst any competing shrubs or trees in the vicinity have been consumed in the conflagration. It's a neat trick if you can pull it off.

NATURE'S LESSON

Being a twisted fire-starter may turn not out to be the ill-considered career move it at first seems.

LIMPET

It cannot be denied that the quality of clinginess is not highly valued in today's society. A person who is said to cling on to another 'like a Limpet' is likely to find themselves scorned or pitied or, where things have gone a bit far, the subject of a restraining order. This is all rather unfair on the tiny dome-like, intertidal gastropod, which the kangaroo court of public opinion has declared guilty by association with the overly dependent. Contrary to popular belief, although Limpets are prodigiously good at staying in one spot despite being lashed by thousands of waves on a daily basis, they can actually move about under their own steam. If they're really in a hurry (when running away from a predatory Starfish, say) they can motor along at a breakneck three inches per hour. They also create little paths on rock surfaces by grazing on Algae and then use these same trails to find their way home again. A Limpet's radula (a sort of tongue) has teeth so hard that they can sculpt rock, a skill it uses to produce a bed to fit its own particular dimensions. These teeth are the Limpet's crowning glory, for they hold a world record amongst living things. Formed on a continually moving conveyor belt, they possess the greatest tensile strength of any known biological material, including Spider silk.

NATURE'S LESSON
You do not have a conveyor belt of teeth. Brush twice daily.

SLEET

It can be fairly safely assumed that no one in the history of
Human vocal communication, outwith the realm of sarcasm, has
ever uttered the expression, 'Oh look, it's sleeting – how lovely.'
There's even some debate over the definition of the word. For
the Americans, Sleet is partially melted droplets of ice, while the
English-speaking nations of the Commonwealth prefer the proper
definition: precipitation comprising rain and partially melted Snow
(though one imagines it's not a word very often used in anger
in Jamaica). The least beloved of all the non-extreme weather
conditions, Sleet appears to possess none of the saving graces of
Rain or Snow, preferring instead to combine the least appealing
aspects of both. However, there is something rather wonderful about
how it is formed. Snow must begin its descent from the clouds when
the lowest reaches of the atmosphere have attained a temperature
a shade above 0°C for a depth of between 750 to 1,500 feet. Vary the
temperature or depth by too much either way and the precipitation
will fall as mere Snow or Rain. On reaching the ground, Sleet rarely
floods people out of house and home, as is sometimes the case with
Rain; nor is it the stuff of avalanches. Rather it is an instant form of
Slush, a much-maligned substance that seldom causes anyone any
serious mischief. There's something rather admirable about that.

NATURE'S LESSON

Setting yourself up as the compromise candidate may not always
win you friends.

DEADLY
NIGHTSHADE

Families are curious things. Take the Solanaceae. Tomatoes, Potatoes and Peppers are all members of that family and all, in their own way, delightful. But there's a whole group of very common and far shadier relations that none of the Solanaceae care to talk about. They are the Nightshade brothers: Woody, Black and, most toxic of all, Deadly. *Atropa belladonna*, as Deadly Nightshade is known to the police, also goes by the aliases Sorcerer's Cherry, Murderer's Berry and Witches' Berry (the placement of the apostrophe suggesting that witches only use it when conspiring together, which is comforting). One of the western hemisphere's most poisonous plants, it sports unremarkable oval leaves, purple-ish bell-shaped flowers and red berries that ripen to an appropriately sinister black. However, the berries are not as poisonous as the leaves, which, in turn, are not as deadly as the roots. It's horrifying, then, to discover that women of the Italian court in the 15th century used a tincture of 'belladonna' (actually atropine, the poisonous element in Nightshades) to make their pupils dilate, thus making them more beautiful – 'belladonna' being the Italian for 'beautiful lady'. More wondrous still is the fact that it's used today by optometrists for the same purpose (if not the same end).

NATURE'S LESSON

What doesn't kill you actually makes you imperceptibly more attractive, albeit only if you're a woman and only within the established conventions of beauty as determined by the patriarchal 15th-century Italian court. So Nietzsche was sort of right.

BAT

Notorious for their love of a good belfry, or indeed any sort of belfry, Bats do not get the press they deserve. For a start, they are indelibly associated with vampires merely because one notable Latin American species (*Desmodus rotundus*, if you're taking notes) happens to bite livestock while they sleep and then laps up their blood. That leaves over 1,200 Bat species which get by on insects or fruit and which leave livestock well alone – which is more than you can say for Humans. And let's not get started on all the Dracula business and that shape-shifting nonsense – almost no one shape-shifts into a Bat any more, and if they do, they do it ironically. In reality, Bats do a great deal of good in the world. For one thing, they pollinate more than 500 plants, including several species of Cocoa, Banana, Mango and Agave (the Cactus from which tequila is derived). They also do a fair bit of seed distribution on the side, for which they receive very little thanks. And while the old English name for a Bat was 'Flittermouse', they're actually more closely related to Humans than they are to Mice. Furthermore, it took *Homo sapiens* until 1906 to devise a form of sonar. Many Bat species, meanwhile, have been using far more sophisticated echolocation techniques for as long as they can remember. Indeed, longer than that.

NATURE'S LESSON

Bats are the only mammals that can properly fly. It's gone way past the year 2000 and we still haven't got personal jetpacks. Stay humble.

CARRION CROW

There are so many folk myths about Crows that if there were a specialist shop that sold only material relating to folk myths, they'd have to give over several shelves to Crow-related ones. And probably part of the 2-for-1 table too. In many cultures they are bringers of bad luck or even harbingers of death. The Ancient Greeks went about cursing one another all day with the phrase, 'Go to the Crows!' And of all the collective nouns we could have chosen, 'a murder of Crows' seems unnecessarily harsh, particularly when Carrion Crows, as the name suggests, prefer their meat served ready-killed rather than going to all the bother of slaughtering their fellow creatures. This is one of the many ways in which Crows display their highly developed intelligence, a trait they share with all Corvids. Scientific studies have shown that they can conspire with one another, hold grudges, and memorise the pattern of traffic lights (so they don't get killed when dropping unshelled Walnuts in front of cars in order to open them). They not only use tools but also use tools to make other tools. Crows can even remember individual Human faces and recall whether the people they belong to have helped them in the past or caused them harm. Basically, they have pretty much all the cognitive skills of Humans. But since 90 per cent of Human activity consists of taking photographs of food to put on Instagram, that's perhaps no longer much of a compliment.

NATURE'S LESSON
If we voted Crows into office instead of Humans, we wouldn't be in this mess.

COMMON
CUCKOO

Can there be a more feckless parent than the Cuckoo? Every year, the female lays between one and two dozen eggs, placing each one in the nest of some other bird: Reed Buntings, Meadow Pipits and Dunnocks are the most favoured targets. She pushes one egg out of each nest in order to make room for her own and to ensure that the numbers tally. And that's it – that's all her parental responsibilities fulfilled. She doesn't even bother building a nest. Meanwhile, the unwitting host parent incubates the egg. When the Cuckoo chick hatches, it flicks out all the other eggs and any chicks that may have hatched (the Cuckoo is born with a dip in its back that helps it scoop them out). The foster parents thus focus all their rearing efforts on the young Cuckoo. This ensures that the literal 'Cuckoo in the nest' gets plenty of food and grows fast, often becoming several times larger than its host parents, which one would have thought would have given the latter pause for thought. After just a few weeks, the fledglings are ready to join their biological parents in Africa. It's no surprise really that this sort of behaviour has made the Cuckoo something of a success – it can now be found in every European country except for Iceland. Needless to say, the male Cuckoo does even less work than the female. He can mostly be found putting his feet up or having competitions with his mates to see which one of them can be heard to call first in spring.

NATURE'S LESSON
Have you ever seen a child? They're basically terrible. Cuckoos have the right idea.

EDIBLE
DORMOUSE

There can be few first names that augur as badly for those christened with it as 'Edible'. Just ask the Edible Frog or the Edible Snail – neither of them are particularly enthusiastic about the moniker. To defend what might otherwise be viewed as a regrettably downbeat outlook on the whole baleful matter of existence, they only have to point to their pitifully low life-expectancy rates. The name was bestowed on this, the largest of all Dormice, on account of the Ancient Roman upper-class practice of keeping them in enclosures to be eaten as a delicacy, baked and stuffed. Alternatively, the unfortunate rodents would be fried so that they might be dipped by patrician fingers into honey and poppy seeds. The fact that the Edible Dormouse is very cute made no impression on their cold Roman hearts. Resembling a smaller, Disney-fied version of a Grey Squirrel (page 110), the Edible Dormouse has short legs, thick light-grey fur, a bushy tail and big, round black eyes. On account of its reputation as a tasty morsel, it has taken to hibernating underground for up to two-thirds of the year. This does rather stretch the meaning of the term 'hibernation', since even the Arctic doesn't go in for eight-month winters. Given all this, it's no wonder the Edible Dormouse prefers to be called by its scientific name, *Glis glis*, which at least only makes it sound like an unbookable tribute act that does covers of Duran Duran in the style of The Glitter Band.

NATURE'S LESSON
While getting drunk may be pleasurable, getting eaten is rarely so.

GNAT

What exactly is a Gnat? Has anyone ever seen a Gnat on its own or are they always in the company of thousands of their fellows? And has anyone the faintest idea what one actually looks like close up? These are good questions and you're probably wishing you'd posed them yourself. So let's go through the answers one at a time. These two-winged insects with hair-thin antennae are true Flies of the order Diptera but all belong to a sub-order of that group called Nematocera, which immediately arouses suspicion. Though they can sometimes be caught having a bit of me time, they do like to swarm about like glorified clouds of floating grit because that's them mating. Looks-wise they more or less resemble a shrunken version of a Mosquito (page 150). Some sorts of Gnats bite, others don't, and even amongst those species that do, only the females bother, and they are certainly not feared like their cousin the Midge (page 138). In short, the Gnat is something of an underachiever. When in the larval stage it will damage crops (particularly Mushrooms), but it rarely causes much more discomfort to humans than that which cannot be eased by a good scratch of the head (or a cough, if half-swallowed). However, they bravely seek to mask their apparently second-rate existence by becoming wildly over-enthusiastic about what's around them. They're attracted to absolutely anything brightly coloured or strong-smelling, while female Gnats will also go mad for carbon dioxide, pot plants and, most mysteriously of all, objects that are jet black, but only if they're moving.

NATURE'S LESSON
Like the world more – it'll make you happier.

COMMON FROG

It's not easy being green, as Kermit so plangently intoned, but that's really the least of the Common Frog's troubles. The fact that it is viewed by enormous quantities of birds, reptiles, fish, small furry mammals and even Hedgehogs as a slow-moving ready-meal is somewhat more unsettling. If that's not enough, Human Beings also get in on the act. Unnecessarily so, one might argue, since they already stuff their faces with a whole smorgasbord of other sentient beings. The French – otherwise amiable types who don't mind how many times you tell them they're incapable of producing any decent pop music despite the fact that they can lay claim to Daft Punk and 50 per cent of the founder members of Stereolab – eat around 4,000 tonnes of Frogs' legs every year. But they're by no means the only offenders. A professor at the National University of Singapore has estimated that up to a billion Frogs per annum are killed for human consumption. Not all of these will be the Common Frog by any means, but it's a figure large enough to make even the most lionhearted among them uneasy. And of course the Common Frogs that get eaten are the lucky ones. They're the survivors of the dangerous frogspawn and tadpole stages when vast quantities of their fellows are devoured, desiccated or destroyed. Also, Common Frogs have permeable skin, which is a downer if you're swimming through water with a load of toxins in it.

NATURE'S LESSON

You may feel your life is unbearably awful but at least the chances of being chewed up by something utterly terrifying and spending your final moments passing into its gut are slim. Try to build on that.

HOUSEFLY

For an insect that neither stings nor bites the Housefly has found many ways of making itself profoundly irritating. There's that ineffectual high-pitched drone for a start, at once weedy and monotonous. It only becomes anything less than ineffably feeble when there are enough of them to make a choir and even then it's merely because the volume has increased – not a single one of them has the wits about them to try droning in a descant. Then there's the constant bumping into things, with that maddening *bzzhzh* noise that occurs on impact. Why do they have to do that? And if Flies' compound eyes, with their thousands of individual visual receptors, are so amazingly effective, how is it that they can't seem to fly for more than three seconds indoors without crashing into something? Then to cap it all there's their disgusting habit of crawling all over the most vomit-inducing faeces they can find before making a beeline for whatever you happen to be eating, as if the two are on the same high-class tasting menu. It's all the more astonishing when you consider that scientists at Trinity College, Dublin, have discovered that the humble Housefly can process information nearly seven times quicker than Humans can. This is why, when you attempt to squash a Fly, it sees you coming in slow motion – it's experiencing time seven times quicker than you are. It observes your pathetically leaden-footed attempts to kill it and it laughs in your face. Then it bumps into your face. Because it wants to.

NATURE'S LESSON
Think quicker, live longer. Also, keep the door shut.

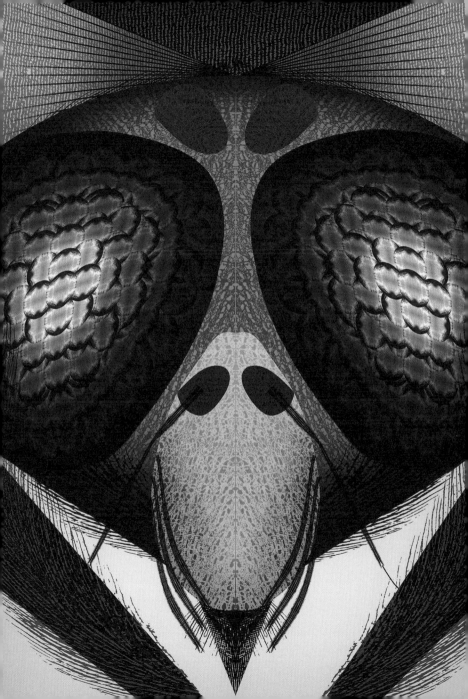

MAGPIE

The Magpie usually builds a roof on its nest; it can recognise itself in mirrors; it has a very memorable scientific name, *Pica pica*. All these things are true. The Magpie is a thief; it is particularly partial to shiny stuff. These things, not so much. The Magpie is no more a thief than we are: it merely assumes that the world is its oyster and takes what it needs. And according to psychologists at Exeter University, Magpies don't like materials that reflect light. Indeed, it turns out they're rather wary of them. It might well be that their reputation as jewellery thieves comes from our need to create a convenient fall guy. Thus, Lady So-and-So hasn't actually fallen on hard times and pawned her jewels, '*a Magpie stole them*'. There's actually a much more significant way in which Humankind and Magpies interact. The former insists on driving over animals on the road in ever-greater quantities and then forgetting to stop to partake of the freshly killed meat, an oversight the Magpie is more than happy to make good. As a result, Magpie numbers have shown a four-fold increase in the last few decades, and the massive surge in the world population of this highly intelligent bird shows no signs of letting up.

NATURE'S LESSON

An old country rhyme accurately interprets what it means when we see a certain number of Magpies: One for sorrow, two for joy / Three for a girl and four for a boy / Five for silver, six for gold / Seven and THE DAY OF THE MAGPIE APOCALYPSE IS UPON US. THIS IS NOT A DRILL.

PUDDLE

Who would be a Puddle? As a body of water it has none of the
grandeur of a Lake nor any of the winsome charm of a Pond. It
seems but an irritant on life's journey, lurking on pavements and
footpaths, in fields and on wasteland (for the Puddle is not proud),
waiting patiently to sodden the foot of the unwary, so to inspire
an unholy tumult of cursings thereafter. Aside from the sun,
young children are its only enemy – the typical infant's insistence
on hurling itself, wellingtons-first, into any little pool of water,
splashing its contents all over the place, has severely curtailed many
a promising Puddle's existence. That's all fine though, right? Well,
no. Puddles, as it happens, act as little oases for the natural world.
No accumulation of water can stay stagnant for very long before
it teems with life. When next you see a Puddle that has evidently
been around for a few days, take a close look into it. The chances
are you'll see microscopic creatures whirling around. Furthermore,
insects including Mosquitoes (page 150) and Dragonflies lay their
eggs in them. Insects are near the bottom of the food chain and
should their numbers collapse catastrophically it would cause a
knock-on effect that would very quickly toll the death knell for
almost all complex forms of life on land, including Humans.

NATURE'S LESSON
Either small children are wilfully ignorant of what they do, or they
are deliberately trying to kill us all. Keep them indoors.

GOAT

Who can tame the Goat? The bovine ungulate ranks among the
most stubborn, wayward and incorrigible animals that Humans
have ever tried to farm. This is not, as might be supposed, because
of its notorious ability to eat absolutely anything (that's a rural
myth, though they do devour many plants that would poison other
animals), but because Goats have proved themselves more than
capable of flourishing in the wild. It's only natural that they should
bridle at any sort of constraint being placed upon their free-
wheeling lifestyle. The Goat has also made an unusually prominent
contribution to the English language. The term 'scapegoat'
arises from the Jewish ritual of Yom Kippur in which one Goat is
slaughtered while another – 'the scapegoat' – is allowed to escape
into the wilderness bearing the sins of the whole nation on its back,
a not inconsiderable feat. The animal is also the star of the phrase 'to
gets one's Goat' which has never, from the very day of its inception,
made any sense at all. And where do you even start on 'acting the
giddy Goat'? Goats are some of the least giddy creatures that ever
roamed the Earth and have a sense of balance and sure-footedness
that almost defies gravity, as any internet search on the phrase
'Unbelievable Mountain Goats' will attest. To these skills can be
added their legendary ability to outsmart trolls. Their only weakness
is their obsession with salt, their need for which can make them go
a bit mental.

NATURE'S LESSON

Goats are the shizz. Even a junkie Goat strung out on salt because
it's been made to carry an entire people's wrongdoings could
hammer your best time on a climbing wall.

SYCAMORE

Not so much a tree as a weed, the Sycamore famously launches its seeds by means of primitive helicopters that propel themselves far and wide. By this method, this quick-growing broadleaf colonises the space around it, potentially creating a drab Sycamore-only monoculture. No wonder conservationists are forever chopping them down and ripping them out to make space for less vilified trees. Even its scientific name, *Acer pseudoplatanus*, sniffily dismisses the Sycamore as a 'fake Plane Tree' as if it were merely a looky-likey rather than a proper plant in its own right. No matter that it can grow up to well over 100 feet and live for more than 400 years – no mean feat for a fake anything. The Sycamore is fiendishly attractive to all manner of Aphids (page 146), which in turn pulls in creatures that enjoy eating Aphids. Small mammals and birds eat its seeds, Bees collect its pollen and Lichen (page 144) just sort of sits on it. And where would the Sycamore Moth be if it did not have a Sycamore's leaves to feed on in its caterpillar stage? The tree also copes well with exposure so gives protection to other species in locations that might otherwise be barren. Humans use its wood to make furniture and kitchen utensils, and Welsh Humans make it into love spoons to sell to tourist Humans. And then there are those rather clever helicopters (actually properly known as samaras) – it took Humankind right up to 1493 and Leonardo da Vinci to come up with a similar concept and hundreds of years more to make one.

NATURE'S LESSON
Even fake things can be quite good (except fake news, which will usher in the end of civilisation).

ANT

If ever a creature got the work/life balance out of whack it is the Ant. Ceaselessly toiling away, always with somewhere to go and a pressing deadline to meet, there's never a moment's rest for the Ant. Yet it is so insignificant that even a Yorkshire Terrier, which is barely even a Dog, might inadvertently crush one underfoot and not notice. It's difficult to believe that Ants are one of evolution's winning teams but there they are, effortlessly carting things about that are 50 times their own body weight. If humans were able to do that, someone who weighed 12 stone could casually wander about with an adult Hippopotamus or one-and-a-half Giraffes tucked under their arm, which would be a boon in certain circumstances. Ants are also capable of farming Aphids (page 146) in order to feed off them; of enslaving other Ants; and of forming up into supercolonies thousands of miles long. Tens of millions of years before Humans took to horticulture, Ants were using dung to increase crop yields and secreting antibiotic chemicals to discourage mould (take that, Alexander Fleming). They're also amazing survivors – it's believed they've been around for 130 million years, so when they started off they were no doubt getting inadvertently crushed under the feet of the Turkey-sized Sinosauropteryx, which was barely even a dinosaur. Were they downcast though? No, they just put their heads down and kept on moving very heavy things from one place to another as if it really mattered.

NATURE'S LESSON

There were dinosaurs as small as Turkeys. No one ever talks about that.

CRAB

A sidler is the Crab. Sidling here. Sidling there. And seldom very subtly or with what one might call *élan*. It's also a bit grabby. One can imagine a parent Crab forever having to tell its offspring not to grab so much at its food, and then, when said progeny saucily replies that the parent also grabs at *its* food, giving the errant child a clip around the basi-ischium. And when they're not sidling or grabbing, Crabs are busy lurking. Admittedly, this they do rather well. Swoosh your fingers through any apparently deserted rockpool and something you thought was a stone or sand or just some sort of non-specific crud will suddenly stir itself and sidle about, and probably have a go at grabbing your fingers into the bargain. But there's so much more to Crabs than sidling, grabbing and lurking. For instance, they can chat amongst themselves, by drumming with their claws or by waving their pincers around, much as Italians would if they had pincers instead of hands. Like the Worm (page 32), Crabs can regenerate themselves if a leg or a claw gets ripped off in a routine scuffle with a Lobster that gets a bit out of hand. By using small electric shocks, scientists from Queen's University in Belfast discovered that Crabs not only feel pain but can remember the experience and attempt to avoid it. And lest it be forgotten, they *can* actually walk slowly forwards or backwards. They only go sideways when they need to get somewhere in a hurry. It just so happens that they're often in a hurry.

NATURE'S LESSON
Like the Crab, you feel pain and are often in a hurry. Unlike the Crab you cannot regrow limbs. Look both ways before crossing.

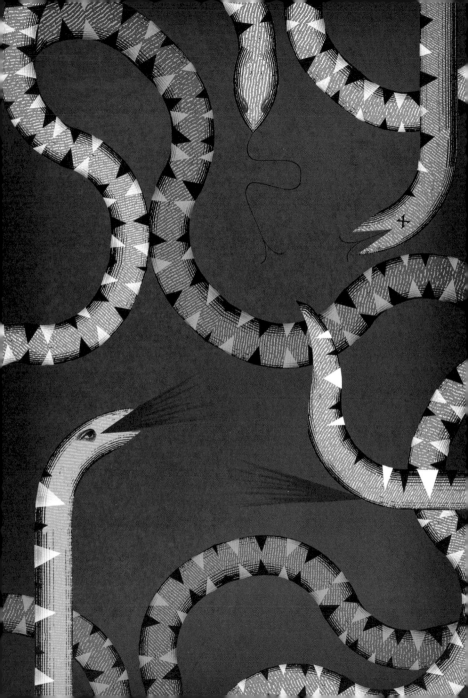

GRASS SNAKE

The Grass Snake is too often viewed as a sort of feeble version of an Adder. Despite the not immaterial detail that the female of the species can grow to over six feet long (making the Grass Snake by far the largest reptile in Britain, a nation teeming with cold-blooded creatures) and is thus larger than its Eurasian cousin, the fact that it is not venomous has led to it being held in a certain amount of unwarranted contempt. No doubt on account of its inability to poison its opponents, the Grass Snake has come up with some admirably cunning dodges when it looks like its number is up. At first it will play dead, sometimes giving itself a nosebleed for added effect. Should this not do the trick, it will seek to disgust its foe by emitting a noxious material from its anal glands that smells like garlic, but not in a good way. Should that not deter the aggressor, it will try hissing and then headbutting it repeatedly. As a last resort it may simply be violently sick. No doubt the Grass Snake is counting on the difficulty its adversaries may have in maintaining their self-respect while eating an animal that's in the process of puking everywhere. Since the Grass Snake has many predators, ranging from Herons and Owls to Foxes (page 14) and domestic Cats, it can expect to go through this ghastly process several times before it's unfortunate enough to find an antagonist so hungry that none of the above will put it off its dinner. In lighter moments, the female lays eggs. Like a Chicken.

NATURE'S LESSON
Die hard.

GRASS

None of us likes to be walked over. And being literally walked over is rarely an occasion for rejoicing either. So just imagine how Grass feels. A family of extremely successful plants that covers around 30 per cent of the globe is nowadays too often reduced to the menial rôle of filling in all the bits of garden that aren't flower beds, paths, vegetable patches, decking or 'that area of cement that Dennis was going to build a shed on before he had his accident'. It wasn't always that way. The first seeds of calamity were sown in the 16th century by French and English aristocrats who developed the concept of the lawn. Even then their preference was to use Chamomile or Thyme. It was only a matter of decades, though, before Grass came into vogue, scythed excessively low by teams of gardeners to produce a verdant, springy platform for the dainty feet of their wealthy masters. The invention of the lawnmower in 1830 by Edwin Beard Budding of Stroud, coupled with the explosion of suburbia wrought by mass industrialisation, made ownership of a patch of closely cropped Grass the all-compelling dream of the Middle Classes. The eternal struggle for the ever tidier and greener lawn had begun. The industrial-military complex was only too happy to supply the necessary carcinogenic chemicals.

NATURE'S LESSON

Lawns are a bourgeois construct that should be resisted by the Masses at all costs. Bring down the Idle Classes by letting the Grass grow wild. Also, it will peeve your neighbours, who are not only the running dogs of Capitalism but also play *The Best of Coldplay* on a Sunday morning.

BINDWEED

'A weed is just a flower in the wrong place,' so the old saying goes. No one actually believes that when faced with a weed in real life, of course, and the fact that we've gone to the trouble of inserting the word into Bindweed's name means that it has little hope for redemption. It doesn't help that Bindweed is such a pernicious character, crowding out or smothering other plants. But much against the odds, these Convolvulus members of the Convolvulaceae family do have some redeeming features. For one thing, they do ceaseless work brightening up the countless brownfield sites Humans litter about the place. Furthermore , should the mood take you, the root of Field Bindweed can be used as a laxative or a purgative. It can also serve as a diuretic, which gives the latter half of the name Bindweed a whole new meaning. To cap it all, the Calystegia members of the Convolvulaceae (it gets no easier with repetition) are so in awe of Bindweed that they have formed their own tribute act: False Bindweed, of which there are at least 25 variants.

NATURE'S LESSON

Education gets everywhere. All climbing Bindweed species wind anticlockwise. If you can't remember which way a clock's hands move, all you have to do is examine some Bindweed and remember that a clock works in the other direction. Suddenly you're a lot better informed and will feel confident and relaxed at dinner parties when the subject arises.

COMMON TOAD

The Common Toad could so easily have gone the same way as its larger brother from another family, the Common Frog (page 66). Sharing the same basic flesh-heavy/bone-light make-up, they too could have become the instant snack *du choix* of a whole alphabet of hungry life forms had they not decided to take preventative measures. When in peril, *Bufo bufo* secretes an irritating toxin called bufagin from glands behind its eyes. It's just a pity that the discharge doesn't entirely deter Grass Snakes (page 82) or Hedgehogs, or indeed certain birds, Rats (page 30) and domestic Cats. Still, at least the Toad is giving it a go. It's the female Common Toad that has it really tough, though. At breeding times their mortality rates are woefully high due to accidental suffocation by a writhing mass of males all attempting to mount a single female at the same time. The resultant 'mating ball' looks as unpleasant as it sounds. Unsurprisingly, around 40 per cent of females give breeding a miss every other year. But perhaps the greatest indignity visited upon the little amphibian is being licked by teenagers in thrall to the urban myth that they can attain some sort of high through doing so. However, if the Common Toad does manage to avoid bufagin-immune predators, is not asphyxiated by its mates and is not licked to death by some misguided yoof, it can potentially live for up to 40 years, by which time it welcomes oblivion with open forelimbs.

NATURE'S LESSON

If you're going to secrete an irritating toxin from behind your eyes, make it really irritating. If Herons, Cats and teenagers still find you attractive, it needs some work.

NETTLE

A plant with an unhappy reputation is the Nettle. Humans will insist on brushing against them and crying out in an aggrieved and rather whiny manner. We cannot say, however, that we have not been warned. That mighty mass of leaves sporting the serrated edges of a saw – that's the Nettle's way of telling other world users to leave it alone. When that warning goes unheeded it's left with little choice but to sting the reckless interloper who has chosen to invade its personal space. The Nettle's hairs snap at the slightest touch, acting like a hypodermic needle to inject a heady cocktail of poisons into the skin, including serotonin, histamine and formic acid. That's not to say that the plant doesn't have a caring side too. It hosts and feeds the larvae of butterflies such as Red Admirals and Small Tortoiseshells. A large Nettle can also churn out up to 40,000 seeds a year, thus providing a banquet for birds. In days of yore, the outer bark-like layers of Nettle stems were used to make cloth and ropes. Indeed, you can go on courses today that will show you how to do just that, so you can be better at pretending you're in the past. There are even books that will tell you how to make Nettle Soup. They're probably the best books you can buy and are written by authors whose interminable penury has made them a master of the dish.

NATURE'S LESSON
Nettle Soup
i Fry an onion with a drop of sunflower oil.
ii Add vegetable stock, season and bring to the boil.
iii Drop in Nettles and simmer for one minute.
iv Blend and serve piping hot, taking care not to spill any over your fast-retreating friends.

'IMA

WORLD

SAUER

NE A

WITHOUT

RAUT. '

STAG BEETLE

There's something uniquely stomach-churningly horrifying about
the Stag Beetle. Everything can feel right about the world: the sun
can be shining, the scenery can be beautiful, the person you're with
can be out of your league but inexplicably slumming it and then
suddenly a Stag Beetle scythes awkwardly past you like a bus that
has been catapulted into the air by mistake, making a noise like
a pack of cards being riffled while threatening you in a plausibly
deniable way. All at once the clouds cover the sun, the scenery feels
dystopian and the scales fall from the eyes of your belovéd. With
its multi-sectored body, glossy wing cases and (in the male's case)
huge black antler-like mandibles, the Stag Beetle looks like a villain
out of an old Marvel comic. It acts a bit like one too – it can spend
up to seven years living as a larva in an underground lair before it's
transformed into the extraordinary beast that it is. Male Stag Beetles
crawl out of the earth around mid-May, a week before the females.
They spend the next three months flying about imitating packs of
cards, fighting other males, mating and then (usually) dying. By
contrast, the adult life of the female (a bit smaller, no mandibles) is
filled with pathos. Though she's able to fly, she mostly just wanders
about. Having mated, she returns to the very same spot where she
surfaced three months beforehand. She takes a final look at the
world, burrows back into her hole, lays her eggs and dies alone.
If her life were a Hollywood film, there wouldn't be a dry eye in
the house.

NATURE'S LESSON

Put off being a grown-up for as long as possible. Arrested
development is the new orange is the new black.

THISTLE

Australia went for a Golden Wattle, Finland opted for Lily of the Valley, while Syria selected Jasmine. It's undeniably a plucky move by the Scottish to choose as their national flower a plant with sharp prickles that's widely viewed as a weed. To be fair though, theirs is the earliest-known example of a national flower – it dates back to the 1200s and King Alexander III – so it's likely they didn't realise that you could choose nice ones as well. Since Scotland has several varieties of native Thistle – the Cotton, Musk, Spear and Melancholy among them – no one's quite sure which one is the actual national flower, which goes some way to explaining why the Scots always look so puzzled. A single Musk Thistle can produce 120,000 seeds, which is excellent news if you're the sort of person who likes a lot of Musk Thistles. The Melancholy Thistle was anything but – according to herbalist Nicholas Culpeper, 'The decoction of the thistle in wine, being drunk, expels superfluous Melancholy out of the body and makes a man as merry as a cricket.' This had nothing to do with the wine, of course. The Roman nobleman and scientist Pliny the Elder believed the Milk Thistle had the power to restore hair, while mediaeval healers used it on patients who suffered with vertigo, jaundice or both. The Thistle's greatest glory though comes from its rôle as a muse. In 1926, the flower inspired Hugh MacDiarmid to write his 2,685-line Scots-language stream-of-consciousness piece *A Drunk Man Looks at the Thistle*, which is now regarded as a masterpiece of modernist poetry.

NATURE'S LESSON

Add a Milk Thistle to a bottle of wine. Neck the bottle.
Look at the Thistle.

SHEEP

Let's face it – we don't much rate Sheep. We find them unintelligent, we think they look at us oddly, and our language is deeply Sheepist. We insult the timid by calling them 'Sheepish'; we tell those who offer blind allegiance that they 'follow like Sheep'; and we call our renegade and mutinous relations 'the black Sheep', not caring for a second to praise all the goody-goody 'white Sheep' of the family. It's only when we come to 'separating the Sheep from the Goats' (page 74) that Sheep come off well, and that's only in comparison to an animal we get cross with because it refuses to do our bidding. It's difficult not to draw the conclusion that this says a lot more about us than it does about Sheep. After all, they were getting on well enough without us. Some indeed still do. There are wild flocks of Soay Sheep on the islands of St Kilda and Lundy, and Moulflon Sheep all over the place from the Caucasus to Corsica. They're not only intelligent (they know how to self-medicate and have an IQ almost as high as pigs) but have emotional intelligence too. For example, they have best friends and become distressed when other Sheep they're particularly close to are taken away or die. They've also been found to recognise 50 faces of their fellow Sheep and remember them two years later, which is probably 50 more than Humans could manage. Basically, everything we think about Sheep is wrong. Apart from the bit about them looking at us oddly. They're definitely doing that. But then why wouldn't they?

NATURE'S LESSON
Count Sheep, not war.

JELLYFISH

We make a big deal about Jellyfish being so darned watery. And it's undeniable: they are on the watery side – between 95% and 98% in truth. But then adult Humans average around 57–60% water and infants can be as much as 78%, which, if you think about it, is kind of hilarious. Small children are basically Puddles (page 72) with a sort of squidgy face attached – no wonder they rarely make sense. Anyway, back with the Jellyfish, or Cnidarians (Greek for 'sea nettle') to give them their proper name. We should really be lauding their desire to keep things uncomplicated. They're no fans of systems, for example: they don't bother with a central nervous system, a respiratory system or a circulatory system. A brain is also deemed surplus to requirements, which is a bold step for any animal. However, with 10,000-odd species drifting about the oceans and one of the longest family trees on Earth – some of their fossilised ancestors are nearly 600 million years old – one can hardly maintain that it's a formula that hasn't worked for them. Sure, some Jellyfish like to mix things up by having eyes, or by being really big (some are larger than Humans), and those varieties that sting possess cells that literally explode on contact with prey or an unwary swimmer's leg, but most recognise that they're just simple plankton, floating about being Zen. It's as well they don't have much of an awareness of time, really, since most of them shuffle off their mortal gastrovascular cavity within a year and particularly tiny ones may only hang around for a few days. Which does rather put everything into perspective.

NATURE'S LESSON
Stay hydrated.

BACTERIA

It's the 21st century and yet we still view Bacteria as our mortal enemy. Come on, people: we should have learnt this one by now. And yet there we go, spraying every surface in the home with products that promise to kill 99.9 per cent of Bacteria (or 'germs' as we prefer to have it, in a bid to sanitise the slaughter and justify it to ourselves, as if our housework were merely a domestic version of the War on Terror which, for future reference, isn't going to end well either). Since we ourselves probably have roughly the same number of Bacteria living in and on us as we have body cells (about 10 trillion if you're an adult), an attempt to wipe out the ones that just happen to be minding their own business on a kitchen worktop is a curiously futile act, even for a Human. Of course, there are Pathogenic Bacteria who can quite happily make us very ill or even kill us, and often do. *Mycobacterium tuberculosis*, for example, sees off roughly two million Humans every year (and snuffed out the all-too-brief candles of Jane Austen and Emily Brontë). Cholera, leprosy, salmonella, tetanus, diphtheria, typhoid and even syphilis and bubonic plague are all gifts from Bacteria to Humankind. However, none of these malaises can be avoided by spraying a liquid in a kitchen. Conversely, there are plenty of Bacteria without whom we would die. All hail *Lactobacillus acidophilus* and its 80 or so *Lactobacillus* chums who help us digest food. And if it weren't for Bacteria we'd have no vitamin K, or indeed sauerkraut. Imagine a world without sauerkraut!

NATURE'S LESSON
Cleanliness is next to oddliness.

PIGEON

In common with so many of our fellow species on this whirling orb, the so-called 'Rat with wings' has attracted the ire of Humans simply because it has been successful. What's more, its curséd ubiquity in our cities is entirely of our doing. We drove the Rock Dove (which is what a Pigeon is) from its natural habitat on the coast by our remorseless hunting. In response, it headed for the city where tall buildings replicated its former cliff-side accommodation. There the Pigeon wreaked a terrible vengeance by outbreeding Humans, dining on their cigarette butts and turning their streets paved with gold into streets paved with guano. Back in the late Middle Ages such a patina of excreta would have been almost as valuable as gold dust, since the saltpetre contained within it was an essential element of gunpowder and could be obtained from no other source. So began the Pigeon's involuntary involvement in wars whose outcome the creature could not have taken the slightest of interest in. Carrier Pigeons played a vital communications rôle in both world wars, with many thousands losing their lives. When not being blown to pieces, Pigeons can find their home from over 500 miles away. The precise manner in which they carry out this wondrous feat remains a mystery. Given how intelligent Pigeons are (they have no problem identifying all the letters of the alphabet and could probably turn them into darn fine poetry if they had a mind to), it wouldn't be at all surprising to discover that they're expert mental cartographers simply because 'they find that kind of stuff easy'.

NATURE'S LESSON
Save money – be your own satnav.

HEAD LOUSE

The devotion that Head Lice harbour for the Human race is touching. They eschew the Dog, the Cat, the Frog, the Bat, the Sow, the Cow, the Kangaroo – only Human blood will do. Head Lice cannot fly and, though they have six legs, they cannot jump, which is pretty feeble. They therefore have to rely on people rubbing their hair against each other in order to spread. Children, being a bit simple, love to engage in this practice, which explains the popularity of the Head Louse at primary schools. Perennially described as being the size of a sesame seed – that well-known indicator of scale – the Head Louse has risen through the ranks to become one of the commonest Human parasites on the planet, up there in the pantheon of the greats alongside the Tapeworm (page 136) and the Mosquito (page 150). The secret of its success has been its ability to emit a waterproof glue, a skill evolution has failed to bestow upon Humans thus far, despite the obvious benefits. The Head Louse uses the adhesive to stick its eggs onto shafts of hair, creating bonds so strong that only a highly trained battalion of nit nurses can separate one from the other. However, climate change may well be on course to wipe out a third of all the Earth's parasitical species – including the Head Louse – by 2070. Their disappearance from the world's ecosystems is likely to make everything go bad. Also, nit nurses will be out of a job.

NATURE'S LESSON
Host a Head Louse, save the planet (and a nit nurse). If that sounds like too much work, jump on the bandwagon and die by 2070.

LUGWORM

Neither syllable of the Lugworm's name is designed to conjure up a vision of loveliness. To be honest, only fans of unevenly segmented tubes that have orifices at both ends are likely to take to the Lugworm's stylings. As it is, the vast majority of us know the Lugworm only by its casts – those rather fun squiggly piles of sand that litter many a beach at low tide. This makes the Lugworm one of those rare creatures that is less physically attractive than its own faeces. But look a little closer and you'll notice tiny hairs that work as magnificently effective gills, bringing in oxygen that is carried around the Lugworm's extensive vascular system by our old friend haemoglobin. The Lugworm can also create its own little waves by making a shuddering motion. This forces water through its burrow and keeps the sand around it nice and soft. No wonder W. B. Yeats included the Lugworm in his poem *The Man Who Dreamed of Faeryland*. The subterranean *Arenicolida* inspired the poet to the heights of lyricism, rhyming 'place' with 'race' and 'mouth' with 'south', thus cementing his position as Ireland's greatest-ever poet.

NATURE'S LESSON

Rejoice. No matter to what degree one's face may be 'made for radio', there's not a Human on Earth who is less attractive than their excreta. Physically, at least.

GREY SQUIRREL

While the Pigeon (page 104) is dismissed as a 'Rat with wings', its fellow city dweller, the Grey Squirrel, is often characterised as a 'Rat with good PR'. And while it's true that they displace Red Squirrels, that's not because they scare their smaller cousins away – they're simply better at life: they out-compete Reds by eating more on the forest floor and by being able to digest acorns. Contrary to popular belief, their acute sense of smell and excellent spatial awareness also makes them very adept at finding the secret caches of nuts they put by for lean times. Furthermore, they can tell whether it's worth their while to open a particular nut simply by picking it up. If the nut is not as heavy as it should be for its size, the Squirrel will reject it. This is a skill Humans have yet to master, despite the fact that most of them will, for reasons lost in the mists of time, spend a large part of each Christmas cracking nuts. Unlike most Humans, Grey Squirrels are almost completely colour blind: they can detect yellows, but everything else is merely a shade of grey. This is why, when you're sitting on a park bench and you get a banana out, Squirrels get excited and start pointing.

NATURE'S LESSON

Next time you go to the park, first cover yourself in custard. This will not only introduce some much-needed colour into the life of a Grey Squirrel, it will cheer you up too.[1]

[1] Definition of what is cheery open to interpretation. Terms and conditions apply.

HORSEFLY

What's more fun than a Housefly (page 68) that just flits about being generally annoying? Why, a Fly that can bite you and cause a host of thrilling side-effects, of course. The Horsefly is probably everyone's least favourite Fly simply because its bites are so famously painful. What's much less well known is that the male Horsefly can reach speeds of up to 90 miles per hour, making him possibly the fastest flying insect on Earth. But it's those bites that grab all the attention. They're the work of the female Horsefly who, in her defence, needs the blood to produce eggs. Her fearsome mouthparts include what look like triple-bladed scissors next to a sort of sponge that soaks up the freshly shed gore. The tear-and-suck method is all her own and is the secret behind the devastation she can leave in her wake: rashes, swelling around the lips and eyes, dizziness, shortness of breath and, in the case of smaller animals bitten many times, death through blood-loss. Known as the Gadfly in times of yore, the Greek playwright Aeschylus has one tormenting Zeus's mistress Io (who has been turned into a Cow, which was one of the dangers of living in Ancient Greece). Shakespeare mentions the Gadfly twice, in *Antony and Cleopatra* and *King Lear*, with the insect acting as a metaphor for something or other, or perhaps just there to make up the syllables because those iambic pentameters didn't fill themselves, you know.

NATURE'S LESSON

No one cares how fast you are. Causing pain is the only way to make people think of you as a metaphor for something. Best not to ask them for what, though.

WEASEL

Few are the complimentary things said of the Weasel. Indeed, while even the Fox (page 14) is praised for its cunning, the Weasel is associated with only negative traits in Humans. Peruse the entry for 'Weasel' in a thesaurus and you'll be bombarded with a cavalcade of unpleasantness, from 'scoundrel' and 'wretch' to 'scuzzball', 'blackguard' and 'varlet'. And yet what has the Weasel done to deserve such opprobrium? Perhaps we take exception to its diet, which largely consists of small furry animals we quite like, such as Voles and Rabbits. Maybe it's the Weasel's shape we don't trust – so thin and long and Snake-like, only with legs and a tail. Or it might just be that we have been infected by the gamekeeper's loathing for an animal that dares to take a Pheasant (page 140) or two before they can be blown out of the sky at point-blank range by a collection of scoundrels, wretches, scuzzballs, blackguards and varlets. Whatever the reason, it's a mystery as to why the Weasel should be so abhorred while its close relative the Stoat suffers no such vilification. This is especially odd given that most people find it impossible to distinguish between the two, despite the fact that the Stoat is much larger than the Weasel, has a black tip to its tail, and turns white in winter in snowy regions. Of course, the proper answer to anyone who asks how to tell them apart is: 'Weasels are weasely recognised while Stoats are stoatally different,' a phrase that has been entertaining young and old for thousands of years.

NATURE'S LESSON
Weasels are weasely recognised while Stoats are stoatally different.

CLOTHES MOTH

Excitingly, there isn't just one Clothes Moth but a wide variety of species whose larvae dine on our attire. The most widespread of these are the Common Clothes Moth (*Tineola bisselliella*) and the familiar faun-coloured Case-bearing Clothes or Carpet Moth (*Tinea pellionella*). Theirs is a world perpetually clouded by grief, for the female dies immediately after laying her eggs. The exercise can take three weeks and involve up to 400 eggs so it's little wonder that she sparks out. The motherless eggs hatch into larvae after a few days. This swift start is followed by a long period of arrested development with the Clothes Moth remaining at the larval, clothes-chomping stage for several years. It means that the little chap or chapess who consumed your favourite jumper last winter may be the very same one who has just devoured those leather trousers that you looked so good in. The good news is that Clothes Moths are ardent carnivores: show them some silk, fur, leather, mohair, cashmere, wool or the like and they'll wolf it down. It means that if you stick to cotton, linen and synthetic garb, you should be safe, assuming you haven't sweated too much into them or drunkenly smeared them with a kebab. Also, note that the case-bearing moth *Coleophora albicosta* feeds exclusively on Gorse (page 48). If you have nothing at all in your wardrobe that's made of Gorse, you can welcome it into your bedroom with the lightest of hearts.

NATURE'S LESSON

You have too many clothes. And those leather trousers? Let a friend tell you – the Moth's done you a favour there.

HERRING GULL

The Herring Gull is a bully. *Larus argentatus* can often be seen swaggering along the street looking for a business to extort or a small child to kidnap. Even when out of sight, Herring Gulls make their presence known by their infamous cry of *Key-owk! Key-owk!*. That's the sound that makes you realise you're at the seaside (assuming the distinctive aroma of stale amusement arcade *à la vinaigrette* hasn't given it away). Unless, of course, you happen to hear a Herring Gull inland and it's just making you feel like you're at the seaside in a bid to disorientate you so it can steal your PIN codes and rinse your bank accounts. However, the Herring Gull's aggressive behaviour is at its most expressive in the matter of defecation. They can excrete on the wing and the sheer volume of material ejected in a single volley makes their attacks akin to carpet bombing. It's a tactic they're more than willing to use, particularly if they feel their offspring are under threat, and gives a whole new meaning to the term 'offensive weapon'. Perhaps more surprisingly, Herring Gulls use both their voice and their body language to communicate with each other in really quite sophisticated ways. And yet, despite employing many of the methods required for surviving in a brutal world – intimidation, theft with menaces, excellent comms – numbers of Herring Gulls are in decline. Boo to that.

NATURE'S LESSON

Nature may be 'red in tooth and claw' but if your particular red is just tomato ketchup you might be in trouble. [NB As of 2015, banks no longer pay out if you give your PIN code away to any seabird smaller than a Gannet.]

WILD BOAR

The nocturnal woodland-dwelling beast with the curved razor-sharp canine teeth that poke out of its lower jaw like tusks is rarely considered beautiful. It was once thought useful, though: until the 1930s its hair was employed as the bristles of toothbrushes, despite the fact that it retained moisture and thus provided a pleasant home for Bacteria (page 102). In common with the Human male, Wild Boar communicate by grunting and releasing various odours from their bodies. However, their young are the sweetest thing imaginable – the wee little piglets are striped and look like tiny Zebras. They and their parents are the untamed ancestors of today's farmed Pig. As such, they share the Pig's intelligence, adding a layer of wisdom on top – most notably the wisdom not to be imprisoned, executed and eaten. In the instances where that might have been its fate, the animal has proved itself an adept escapologist. The sounders of Wild Boar living in the wild in various parts of Britain are the result of numerous escapes from Wild Boar farms and, even more spectacularly, an abattoir. In tribute, 1980s popular beat combo Duran Duran had a top-ten hit about the animal. Though a catastrophic typographical error at the printers meant that the single was mistitled 'Wild Boys', even a cursory listen will verify that lead warbler Simon Le Bon is actually singing 'Wild Boars'. His assertion that 'Wild Boars always shine' is clearly a reference to the glossy nature of the creature's bristly coat and its tendency to glisten when flecked with rainwater.

NATURE'S LESSON
Check everything that comes back from the printers.
They do it deliberately, you know.

FUNGUS

There's a reason why 'I have a fungal infection' is not a winning phrase on a first date. Nobody loves a Fungus. They have no brain, no sense of who they are (as far as we know) and are lovers of dank, dark, rotting places – just the kind of locations we do our best to avoid. Also, there are at least 300 that are poisonous to Humans, which is not the sort of behaviour that endears them to us. But the next time you go into a wood, you might want to say 'thanks' to our unloved friend. As unlikely as it may sound, Fungi form the telephone network by which trees communicate with each other. It's a function of what is known as Mycorrhiza – a symbiotic relationship between a Fungus and a tree, with the former living on the latter's roots. The Fungus gets some lovely sugars from the tree. In return, the tree benefits from being able to suck up greater quantities of water and minerals through the Fungus. But the really clever thing about this subterranean network of Fungi is that it allows trees to send each other warning signals about attacks by Aphids (page 146). The tree under assault and those receiving the message then release volatile organic compounds which attract creatures that feed on Aphids. Simple, but brilliant (unless you're an Aphid).

NATURE'S LESSON

Do not attempt to communicate with other Humans by means of your fungal infection. Especially if all you've got to say is that you're being attacked by Aphids. Leave it to the second date at least.

DADDY LONGLEGS

Argh! The Daddy Longlegs. There's nothing it enjoys more than
appearing on a beautiful still summer's evening and slamming itself
into someone's face before flying just out of reach, only to repeat
the procedure ten minutes later, just as the victim has regained
some sort of composure. If the Daddy Longlegs is feeling in a really
devilish mood it will follow up this prank by throwing itself leg-long
into the target's Pimm's and lemonade. But they're no snobs – if the
victim happens to be imbibing a glass of their own urine, they will
just as happily throw themselves into that. However, they're not
entirely without self-respect so they do draw the line at Australian
lager. So three cheers for the Daddy Longlegs, aka the Crane Fly, aka
the *Tipulidae* family, aka Gah-what's-that-it's-in-my-eye-I've-gone-
blind-I've-gone-blind-oh-it's-gone-now-sorry. With its freakishly
long spindly legs, fancy transparent wings and ability to pilot itself
through the skies in its sacred quest to freak out Humans, the Daddy
Longlegs outshines its American Arachnid rival, the Harvestman,
aka the Pholcidae family aka... Daddy Longlegs. The fact that two
very different creatures ended up with the same nickname says more
about the apparent limits on Human imagination than perhaps we'd
care to admit. The American version of the True Daddy Longlegs™
boasts an ancestry that goes back over 430 million years, when
it began evolving away from the Scorpion. However, over all that
time it still hasn't learnt how to organise and carry out a successful
bombing raid on a Pimm's. Accept no substitutes.

NATURE'S LESSON
The thing about self-respect and Australian lager. *Obviously.*

SEAWEED

Encounters in the wild with Seaweed are not generally affairs that get mentioned in postcards home. We tentatively pick our way across the slimy coastal morass, slipping and sliding as we go. The large marine Algae we're stepping on is very often Sea Wrack, Carrageen or Purple Laver, though it's likely we'll point to any of those and identify them definitively as Bladderwrack as our kin look on wonderstruck, never knowing they had a naturalist in the family. There are myriad variations of Seaweed, which – as we shall also point out to our relations – is too vague a term for any self-respecting botanist to use. Those Green, Red or Brown Algae that are considered to be Seaweed need just two elements in order to flourish: salty water and sunlight (for photosynthesis). Beyond that, it's a case of evolution doing its thing. As for edible varieties, there's Nori, Dulse, Arame, Wakame and a veritable *sushini* of others, eaten in delicious fresh or dried forms by people in many Eastern Asian countries; and *bara lawr* (laverbread), a stodgy form favoured by the Welsh, who have to spend their lives pretending that boiling Purple Laver – then dipping it in oatmeal and frying it – is just as nice, really, and would you care for some more because there's loads?

NATURE'S LESSON

The Welsh are right about some things (there's space below to make your own list) but trust our Eastern Asian friends on this one.

JAPANESE
KNOTWEED

Rush into a crowded theatre and shout the phrase 'invasive species' and the chances are that, as you're being pulled away by the ushers, you'll hear someone in the audience mutter the words, 'Japanese Knotweed'. Everywhere the plant has gone it has caused so much chaos that one wonders how Japan, whose volcanic slopes are the beast's natural home, has managed to cope. It's surprising then to find that the plant is a member of the otherwise lovely Polygonaceae family, one of whose members, Dock, has been relieving the sting of Nettles (page 90) since time immemorial. There was a time when people thought the world of Japanese Knotweed too. It won awards when it was introduced at Kew Gardens in the mid-19th century and was subsequently used up and down the country to stabilise railway embankments. This was before it was discovered that Japanese Knotweed is more Triffid than triffick. It can grow by up to four inches a day in summer; its rhizomes can produce new plants over 20 feet away from the mother plant; and it has no natural predators. As a result, it's not only illegal to propagate it, you can even run foul of the law by not disposing of its remains correctly. And even if you think you've got rid of it, the chances are you haven't – it typically takes several years of work to eradicate a stand of Japanese Knotweed. It's basically Superman/Wonderwoman in plant form (though, unlike them, it can also be used as a laxative).

NATURE'S LESSON
Come from Japan.

MALLARD

The Mallard is so common that when Samantha from Human Resources sits you down over a Lambrusco and dish of Kalamata olives to talk to you about your imminent sacking but eases into the conversation by relating a story about a walk she had in the park over the weekend during which she saw what she describes as 'a Duck', it will be taken as read by both parties that she means a Mallard. Sadly, such familiarity has tended to breed contempt (which is why Samantha's talking to you in the first place). Although it's true that drakes do have the distressing habit of attempting to mate with a duck en masse, quite often resulting in the drowning of the latter, Mallards as a whole are a worthy lot. For one thing, the chicks don't demand to be fed, as is the case with most other birds. As soon as all the duck's eggs are hatched – the last chick usually emerges within 24 hours of the first – she takes her brood out onto the water and they are henceforth responsible for collecting and eating all their own insects (they become largely vegetarian in later life when they rightly discern that eating insects is a bit revolting). But of course the Mallard's claim to fame is its call, one of the most widely recognised of any animal on the planet. This quack is the preserve of the female. The drake just sort of mumbles, ashamed on account of all the drownings.

NATURE'S LESSON

When Samantha tells you that something is water off a Duck's back, remind her that it's really off a Mallard's back. After all, you won't see her again after the tribunal.

EUROPEAN MOLE

You've got to hand it to Moles; they really enjoy a good dig. I mean, they really enjoy it. Dig dig dig – that's what they like. Show them some earth and they'll knock you up a fine tunnel in no time. If they're really in the mood, or they're having some friends round for supper, they can excavate over 60 feet of tunnel in a single day. This is some feat for a creature measuring a mere seven inches from nose to tail. And just so everyone in the world above knows where they've dug, they proudly leave a little heap of spoil above the surface. The European Mole is not blind, as is often supposed, but understandably doesn't have a great deal of call for seeing things, so keeps its eyes almost entirely covered by fur. And as might be expected for a creature that spends almost its entire life underground, it does not court publicity. However, one particular Mole (whose name has been successfully kept out of the press) was credited with killing a king of England. William III was the victim, dying of pneumonia after breaking a collarbone when his Horse stumbled on a Mole hill. For years afterwards, Jacobites raised a toast to 'the little gentleman in the black velvet waistcoat', which at least gave them something to be cheery about.

NATURE'S LESSON

Do what you love. Go easy on the regicide though.

HOUSE MOUSE

The House Mouse just wants to be our friend. What other reason could there be for its collective decision each year to make its nest in hundreds of millions of homes around the globe if not to propagate Humano-Mousal relations? Sadly, for all its willingness to extend the paw of fellowship and amity, *Mus musculus* rarely finds a welcome in the dwellings it enters. It is poisoned, has its back snapped in half, or is made a plaything by that most trenchant opponent of closer association between Humans and Mice, the domestic Cat. When not being tortured or killed, the House Mouse seizes every opportunity to show off to the homeowner its astounding array of skills. It can make vertical leaps of up to a foot; climb smooth, sheer surfaces as if gravity were an illusion; is a more than competent swimmer should the need arise; and never vomits, despite the fact that it has to eat its own droppings to remain healthy. However, it is the House Mouse's ability to squeeze itself through tiny apertures that is perhaps the one that most astonishes the onlooking Human. Present it with a hole no larger than the end of a pencil and the little rodent will be through it quicker than you can put your hands together to applaud it.

NATURE'S LESSON

Befriend the House Mouse in your life. If you're patient, it may teach you how not to vomit, one of the most highly prized social skills the modern Human can acquire.

TAPEWORM

Does the Tapeworm have a rival among Human parasites? While the Tick (page 34), the Head Louse (page 106) and other blood-sucking creatures hang about on a person's skin, the Tapeworm goes full Mexico and lives right inside the Human digestive system. Over the years they've developed all the skills necessary for life inside a narrow tube packed with fast-flowing ingredients – the chief of which is not getting flushed out. Some use retractable hooks, some go for suckers, while others prefer a series of grooves that form a partial vacuum with the lining of the host's intestines. They're not actually Worms (or indeed made of tape) and to live a full life often need their first host to be eaten by a different host and for that host to be swallowed up by a third host, which takes some organising. They can live in animals as large as Whales – growing to be 100 feet long in some cases – and as small as Beetles. And when it comes to their interaction with Humans, Tapeworms really can say something about an individual's well-being or lack of it. Controversial missionary Bruce Olson once went for so long without food while lying wounded in the jungle that one of his Tapeworms climbed through his stomach, up his throat and poked its head into his mouth in the search for sustenance. More recently, no fewer than 52 Tapeworms were discovered inside a North Korean soldier who had defected to the South. Members of the armed forces, it should be noted, form a relatively well-off segment of North Korean society.

NATURE'S LESSON

Let the Tapeworm be the yardstick of your success in life. If you have fewer than 52 and none of them are starving to death, you're probably doing OK.

BITING MIDGE

Scotland's worst-kept secret also happens to be the worst-kept secret in Scandinavia and northern Canada. No doubt it would also be the worst-kept secret in Siberia and Greenland if they too were thrusting holiday destinations. And that not-so-secret secret is the Ceratopogonidae family's Biting Midge. From May to September clouds of them blot out the sun and play havoc with the nerves of every blood-filled creature below. As is true of the Gnat (page 64), only the female bites. However, attempting to determine the sex of the Midge heading towards your tender skin is not a game for those who wish to remain unbitten. It's little consolation that of the 40 different varieties of Midge in Scotland only five attack Humans. But there is still something to admire about these microscopic fiends of the air. Though barely visible with the naked eye, they can literally sniff out likely victims and have a special saliva that keeps blood from clotting once they've sliced through the skin. Furthermore, they're a major source of food for birds, Bats (page 56) and your second- and third-favourite carnivorous plants, Butterworts and Sundews. Where would we be without them, eh?

NATURE'S LESSON

Biting Midges seek out Humans by homing in on the carbon dioxide we breathe out. If you wish to avoid being bitten, simply restrict yourself to breathing in.

PHEASANT

What a sad and rather pathetic figure the Pheasant cuts. It stalks mournfully through the copses and thickets, eyes cast downwards as if composing some epic tone poem about how terribly tragic, miserable and wretched is this shabby thing we call life. When it takes to the air one can begin to see just why it thinks that way too. No matter how frantically it beats its clipped wings, it rarely manages to climb higher than 20 feet into the sky before it glides back down to earth, exhausted by its short-haul flight. It's a prey species – Humans who pay thousands of pounds for the privilege of shooting them being the major predator – and is also susceptible to inclement weather, so very few Pheasants see their first birthday. They used to hold the record among amniotes (i.e. mammals, birds and reptiles, as any fule no) for having the smallest genome – a mere 970 million base pairs (for comparison, Humans have 3 billion, which is why we're all so fat) – but the Black-chinned Hummingbird's has since been mapped out and discovered to be smaller. That disappointment doubtless fills a few stanzas in the Pheasant's poem. Its one consolation is its extraordinarily beautiful plumage. The male in particular, with his long banded tail, mottled bronze breast, white collar, bottle-green-and-royal-blue neck and red face make him a most striking visitor to the countryside. Indeed, if only the Pheasant were as rare as the Peacock we would surely shower it with praise instead of shot pellets.

NATURE'S LESSON

Some people are the worst-possible people. Don't be one of those.

HOUSE SPIDER

Arachnophobes should really find somewhere else to live other than houses. House Spiders, as their name suggests, like to live in a house themselves. Since it is futile attempting to build a house out of silk, despite that material's legendary strength, they have no other option but to make themselves at home in houses built by Humans. They're staggeringly common, having colonised most of Europe and North America, and if you encounter one it's likely to be a chap. Males are the smaller of the two sexes and must roam about in search of a mate since the females like to build a web somewhere quiet and stay put. In their defence, House Spiders do pay a sort of rent in kind, in that they catch and digest a lot of insects and other creepy-crawlies that Humans are not enthusiastic about having around the house. And one other thing in their favour is that they're not the increasingly widespread and numerous Giant House Spider. The two species share an ancient ancestor, but the Giant House Spider makes its cousin look rather puny and ineffectual by comparison. It's even said that a Giant House Spider can bite a child's face off, but you shouldn't believe everything you read. Sweet dreams.

NATURE'S LESSON
No matter what you do, they will come for you and your end will not be swift.

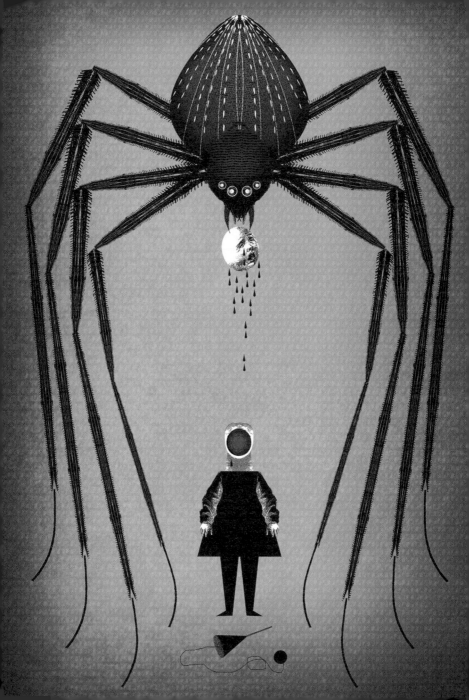

LICHEN

The trouble with Lichen, as John Wyndham might have observed had he downed one sherry too many before settling down to write, is that it just kind of sits there being a bit rubbish. What's more, almost no one can confidently say what a Lichen actually is. Merely stating that they are symbiotic associations between Fungi (page 122) and Algae and/or a Cyanobacteria is all well and good (and actually the truth, which is something to be cherished in today's world) but not terribly meaningful to non-botanists. However, despite – or perhaps on account of – the enigma of their existence, they are phenomenally successful and can be found in thousands of different varieties all around the globe. They may also hold the key to how life on Earth expanded from the oceans to dry land. It seems likely that neither Fungi nor Algae, both of which evolved in the seas, could have made the leap to life on land by themselves but needed each other's assistance to do so. Thus, when you see a Lichen, you are looking at an example of cooperation between a combination of organisms without which life on land would probably not exist. In short, without Lichen there would be no Humans.

NATURE'S LESSON
It's pronounced 'liken'.

APHID

You can sometimes pick up clues about the character of creatures from their collective nouns. Sheep (page 98) amble around in inoffensive flocks. Wild Boar (page 120) trot about in mysterious sounders. Aphids, however, insist on rocking up in nothing less flamboyant than an infestation. It doesn't matter what sort of Aphid they are – Greenfly, Blackfly, Whitefly – they're all disgustingly gregarious. The reason they're never in want of friends, or indeed family, is because the females can usually reproduce parthenogenically. In other words, they can bring forth offspring without all the fuss of mating and can thus throw themselves into the world of single-parenthood at a very tender age, perhaps producing thousands of children over a lifetime. This may all seem like fun and japes but there's a reason why they hang about in such vast numbers: the sheer range and variety of their predators. Aphids are eaten by birds, mammals and other insects; they're poisoned by insecticides; they're squashed to death by enormous green-gloved fingers; and when they're not being farmed by Ants (page 78) they're being blown to smithereens by Wasps (page 26). You'd have thought that seeing everyone you know wiped out in all manner of hideous ways would have got Aphids down but they're very stoical about it, especially the female ones. After all, if they ever run out of friends, they can just give birth to some more.

NATURE'S LESSON

If you have so many friends your crowd is known locally as an infestation, it's time to get rid of some. Insecticide is surprisingly efficient at this, but unfriending them on social media should also do the job.

SHREW

Pity the Shrew: its existence is a bit of a mess. Not only is it one of the favourite meals of a large number of efficient killing machines – Owls, Kestrels, Foxes (page 14), Weasels (page 114) and Stoats all find a bit of raw Shrew delicious – it's also home to a shedload of parasites, so it spends most of its short life (typically less than a year) either being consumed from within or consumed from without. Even its one defence mechanism is hopeless. The Shrew tries to make itself unpleasant to eat by emitting a liquid produced by glands on its skin, but is very often killed by predators such as domestic Cats before they realise that their victim is too disgusting to consume, and so leave the corpse to rot. Then on top of that there's the whole sexism thing: the labelling of women as Shrews if they have the temerity not to be entirely submissive. No matter that the animal is not unusually bad-tempered or aggressive itself. It doesn't help that Shakespeare, notably a man, wrote a whole play about the successful taming of one. It's no wonder women get cross and that the Shrew takes it out on its food, wolfing down roughly its own body weight in insects and Worms (page 32) in a single day. In fact, it's so small (the Pygmy Shrew is one of the tiniest mammals in Europe) and its metabolism so fast that it must eat every two to three hours to avoid dying. It must wonder sometimes whether it wouldn't be easier to do just that and cut out the middleman. The fact that it doesn't should be an inspiration to us all.

NATURE'S LESSON
Men, for goodness sake, sort yourselves out.

MOSQUITO

As your head sinks satisfyingly into the pillow and you deliver yourself gladly into the arms of Morpheus, there is no noise more irritating than the whine of a high-pitched dentist's drill delivered straight into the inner cavities of your ear. Suddenly all thoughts of sweet oblivion are gone – there is a Mosquito in the room. As with the Horsefly (page 112), Gnat (page 64) and Biting Midge (page 138), it's the females that do the biting, all in the name of egg-creation. They're quite the surgeon too, carefully injecting both a painkiller, so you don't feel the bite until after it's happened, and an anticoagulant that enables them to suck your most excellent blood through one of a pair of fine syringe-like mouthparts. The Mosquito's body is semi-transparent so you can actually watch your blood filling her up, if that's what floats your boat. In many countries the Mosquito brings the added delight of a possible dose of malaria, dengue fever, encephalitis, West Nile virus, chikungunya or yellow fever, among other treats doled out by Mother Malaise from her plentiful collection. Indeed, one might almost imagine that she had designed the Mosquito herself because her helpmeet, though so small and weedy-looking, is a stunningly effective bringer of pain, disease and death. It's a Tory cabinet minister in insect form.

NATURE'S LESSON

Mosquitoes born of eggs formed partially from your blood are, in some sense, your children. If they go on to give other people fatal diseases, that's down to your absentee parenting. Maybe it's time you took a long hard look at yourself.

HUMAN

Hominid; biped; one of the more dangerous Apes. The Human considers itself the cleverest of all the creatures on planet Earth despite its continuing widespread inability to understand and use the apostrophe, elect anyone half-decent into any major position of political power, or create a dairy-free cheese that tastes anything like cheese. The Human owes a great deal of its status as the globe's dominant species to the possession of opposable thumbs. These have enabled it to peel bananas (albeit from the wrong end), make Jägerbombs, and take what it calls a 'selfie': a digital image whose dissemination is intended to demonstrate to other Humans that the pictured individual's life is not as wholly meaningless as is generally believed, but which more often than not merely confirms the impression. The Human is a beast of simple pleasures (see Jägerbombs, above) – nothing amuses it more than asking its fellow Humans how many members of a certain community it would take to change a light bulb. When there is no reply, or the hearer responds incorrectly, the questioner then supplies the answer, which it appears they knew all along. Also credited with inventing the Twiglet.

NATURE'S LESSON

Avoid if possible. When not possible, engage in conversation re: the staffing levels required for simple domestic electrical tasks. They seem to like that.

'NOBODY
KNOWS
STICKS
FR

REALLY
WHERE
COME
M.'

INDEX

A

Aeschylus 113
agaves 56
algae 23, 51, 126, 145
ants 32, 79, 146
aphids 27, 76, 79, 122, 146
arame 126

B

bacteria 102
banana plants 56
basil 10
bats 56, 138
bees 27, 76
beetles, stag 94
belladonna 55
bindweed 87
birds 88, 138
   carrion crows 59
   common cuckoos 60
   dunnocks 60
   herring gulls 118
   kestrels 149
   magpies 71
   mallards 130
   meadow pipits 60
   owls 83, 149
   pheasants 114, 141
   pigeons 105
   reed buntings 60
   stonechats 48
   whinchats 48
   yellow-browed warblers 48
birdsfoot trefoil 10
blackfly 146
bladderwrack 126
boars, wild 121
bryophytes 23
Budding, Edwin Beard 84
bufagin 88
butterflies 91
butterworts 138

C

carnations 10
carrageen 126
case-bearing moths 117
cats 83, 88, 134, 149
chikungunya 150
Chilean bellflower 10
clarkia 10
clothes moths 117
cockroaches 11, 12
cocoa 56
convolvulus 87
crabs 80
crows, carrion 59
cuckoos, common 60
Culpeper, Nicholas 97
cyanobacteria 145

D

daddy longlegs 125
dandelions 11, 24
deadly nightshade 55
dengue fever 150
destroying angel 28
diseases
   bubonic plague 102
   chikungunya 150
   cholera 102
   dengue fever 105
   diphtheria 102
   encephalitis 150
   leprosy 102
   Lyme disease 35
   malaria 150
   rabies 20
   salmonella 102
   syphilis 102
   tetanus 102
   ticks 35
   tuberculosis 102
   typhoid 102
   West Nile virus 150
   yellow fever 150
docks (plants) 129
Doctrine of Signatures 9, 10
dormice, edible 63
dragonflies 72

ACKNOWLEDGEMENTS

Books are almost always the work of a team. In the case of *The Wisdom of Nature*, that's particularly true and I'd like to give my heartfelt thanks to **Katie Ponder**, whose wonderful illustrations have kissed my words into joyful things.

I'd also like to show my appreciation to **Molly** and **Pip** for their fine and timely advice on Cockroach knees.

There are several extremely kind people who put me up while I was writing this book and whose homes, in the bosom of Mother Nature, provided much inspiration:

Debs and **Neil** at Broad Meadow House, Charlestown, Cornwall
Kim and **Nick** at Ivy Grange Farm, near Halesworth, Suffolk
Mark, **Jude**, **Seth** and **Silas** at Ergata, near Ingleton, North Yorkshire
Michèle and **Richard** in Montreux and Villaz, Switzerland
Damian and **Renu** in Ceglie Messapica, Puglia, Italy
(Who'd be an author, eh? It sounds terrible.)

I'd like to record my gratitude to my hard-working and patient agent, **Michael Alcock** of Johnson & Alcock.

And finally, a veritable tsunami of thanks goes to my editor, **Céline Hughes**, and everyone else at Quadrille through whose hands this manuscript passes on its way to bookdom. Bless you all.

PUBLISHING DIRECTOR Sarah Lavelle
COMMISSIONING EDITOR Céline Hughes
DESIGNER Maeve Bargman
ILLUSTRATOR Katie Ponder
PRODUCTION DIRECTOR Vincent Smith
PRODUCTION CONTROLLER Tom Moore

Published in 2019 by Quadrille,
an imprint of Hardie Grant Publishing

Quadrille
52–54 Southwark Street
London SE1 1UN
quadrille.com

Cataloguing in Publication Data: a catalogue record for this book is available from the British Library.

Text © Dixe Wills 2019
Illustration © Katie Ponder 2019
Design © Quadrille 2019

ISBN 978 1 78713 222 1

Printed in China